To GLENN & RUTH -

WILDERNESS WISHES

TO YOU!

Showy orchis and friend, Buffalo River Wilderness

Tupelo swamp, Conway County

ARKANSAS PORTFOLIO II

Spectacular New Photos of "The Natural State"

TIM ERNST

CLOUDLAND.NET PUBLISHING

Cave Mountain, Arkansas

www.Cloudland.net

The premium quality of the images in this book are due in part
to the cooperation and great service from the owners and staff of
Bedfords Camera and Video stores located throughout Arkansas.

All of the images in this book are available as fine art prints in a variety of sizes and prices.
They are printed one at a time per your order by Tim Ernst.
Visit the web site for all of the details, and to view other online galleries of Tim's work.

Autographed copies of this book may be ordered direct from Tim Ernst:

CLOUDLAND.NET PUBLISHING
HC 33, Box 50-A
Pettigrew, Arkansas 72752 (Cave Mountain)
870-861-5536
Visit our online store at www.Cloudland.net to see our complete selection
of picture books, guidebooks, posters, and fine art prints.

Quantity discounts available, and new dealers are always welcome.

Several years ago I got rid of all my camera equipment and my camera bag was empty—I had given up taking serious photographs and was content to live out my life in the woods on the sidelines, watching and not recording. Then a beautiful wilderness wildflower arrived and filled my life with love and purpose. She gave me the encouragement I needed to restock my camera bag once again and return to one of my life's greatest passions, capturing the beauty of Momma Nature and sharing it with you. All of the images in this book were taken after I met her, and are the result of her insistence that I get up and get out of bed and go take pictures! So I dedicate this collection to the love of my life, Pamela. Daisies are her favorite wildflower, and thousands of them surround our wilderness cabin each summer, including the ones below.

Sunrise through an old cedar, Buffalo River Wilderness

Contents

Introduction

Welcome to my newest collection of images from Arkansas! The original *Arkansas Portfolio* was my very first picture book, was published in 1994, and is out of print. *Arkansas Portfolio II* is my sixth picture book, and I take great pleasure in presenting the latest vision of my home state to you.

Every image presented here is brand new and has never been published in a book before. They are the result of my recent explorations with camera in hand, to some of my favorite haunts around the state, but also to new locations that I had never been to. Part of my job is finding new scenes for you to look at, and I take that job seriously!

There are waterfalls—lots of thundering waterfalls and gentle cascades; tons of wildflowers that you will get up close and personal with; sunrises and sunsets and moons; and photos of wildlife like you've never seen from me before. There are also photos of old barns, weathered and wonderful and part of the natural landscape; and swamps and mountaintops and mushrooms, oh my.

And for the very first time I present to you a group of unique fine art black and white images. These include infrared photos taken with a specially-adapted digital camera, as well as more traditional images of the black and white landscape.

There are 113 photographs in this collection. They are presented in four groups, but are not organized in any particular way. You can open the book and begin to browse wherever you like. All photos have a brief identifying caption, and most have a little bit of text about how the photo was taken, some interesting tidbit about the subject, or a thought or two about nature. Other images have expanded text of one sort or another (sorry if I get a little long-winded!). There is a short discussion in the back of the book about my photography equipment, plus a complete list of camera and lens used for each photo (I used eight different cameras and 16 lenses for this book project). Don't forget to take a look at the last page!

If you don't have a lot of time, I suggest that you simply turn the pages and look at the pictures. Then when you are ready for the total experience, seek out a quiet place, put on some nice music, get a cool drink, sit back and relax, and come explore Arkansas with me. It is the most magical land on the planet, and I hope this book brings you a little closer to it. Enjoy!

Tim Ernst

Tim Ernst at Cloudland
July, 2005

Early morning light on a frigid winter day, Dug Hollow, Buffalo River Wilderness

Part One

My love affair with wildflowers began a long time ago, and I have photographed thousands of them in Arkansas and all across the United States. In the past I have mostly taken photos from a distance, standing back and showing the flowers and where they live. But recently my technique has been a more deliberate one, and I have moved in closer, much closer, revealing intimate detail and personality of individual flowers. I don't use any sort of artificial light, but will bounce some soft light up into the face of a flower if needed to bring out that detail. And I like dark backgrounds, even black, so that nothing distracts from the flower.

The flower photo at right was taken at the end of a very long day of shooting in the Ouachitas, one in which I photographed many groups of colorful wildflowers. I talk to myself a lot when I am working alone, and after spending a couple of hours with this one particular patch of flowers, I kept telling myself, *OK, that is IT, you got the perfect flower shot, it is time to quit—this is the very last shot!* And so I packed up all my camera gear and got ready to hike out. As I always do these days, after taking two steps down the trail, I stopped, turned around, and looked back at where I had been shooting just to see if I had left anything behind. And then I spotted it—this lovely group of spiderworts all tangled up in a fern, growing within inches of where my camera bag had been sitting all that time. Even though I had many great flower shots already, and the light was fading fast, I got out my camera gear once again and set up this shot. There was a slight breeze blowing, and when you do photos like this one the wind has to be absolutely still or your shot will be ruined. So I sat there, and waited, and waited, and waited, for perhaps fifteen minutes. This job of mine keeps me on my belly in the dirt a lot, but I get to hang out with some remarkable faces of nature. The breezes finally stopped just long enough for me to make this four-second exposure, and it turned out to be the very best shot of the day!

Spiderwort and fern, Caney Creek Wilderness, Ouachita National Forest

October reflections, Buffalo National River

Sometimes the reflections in the water are much more interesting than the original. I spend a lot of time wandering around creeks looking at reflections, especially in the fall when the colors begen to blaze.

Waterfall cascade, Leatherwood Creek, Buffalo National River

Water wants to run and fall and be free. I could sit at the base of a waterfall for hours, letting the cool spray cover my face, while I dream the day away. And I often do.

Dogwood berries holding on to that last drop of rain, Ozarks

If you look really close, you can see the entire world reflected in a single raindrop. I wonder what it looks like from inside that drop of water? How funny I must have looked from in there when I pointed my long macro lens at the drop.

Buzzard Roost Special Interest Area, Ozark National Forest (yup, that's me)

Have you ever felt like an ant? That's what happens when you wander around down inside this unique rock formation. There are numerous tall canyons of solid sandstone that tower high above you, as you scramble around trying to find the way out!

Forked Mountain, Flatside Wilderness Area, Ouachita National Forest

The Ouachitas are covered with pine trees, but they also have a lot of hardwoods that produce blazing colors in the fall. Forked Mountain is a very magical place, and has drawn me to it for more than 30 years; first as a college student, leading backpack trips into the wilderness, and now when I want to photograph a dramatic landscape. I will often come to this viewpoint that is located up on a neighboring hillside and just sit and watch the clouds roll by.

Ice hoodoos, Dug Hollow, Buffalo River Wilderness

These delightful little characters were formed as the water level in this stream went down, and the last drops of water hanging on the underside of the branches froze. More ice was added to each "hoodoo" over time, and they grew. There was a small waterfall just upstream that sent ripples across the pool—it was great fun to watch as the hoodoos (and their reflections) looked like tiny ice dancers that never seemed to touch the ground!

**Fog in the trees,
Upper Buffalo Wilderness,
Ozark National Forest**

If you listen, sometimes the wilderness will speak to you. It will often be in hushed tones, like the sound of fog moving gently through the trees, whispering to you.

The last moonrise before it collapsed, an old barn along Hwy. 21 between Kingston and Boxley

This little barn has always been a favorite of mine, and I have photographed it many times over the years. When it began to lean pretty badly, I stepped up my efforts to catch the full moon rising behind it at sunset, when the barn and field and trees would be glowing. I managed to catch everything just right—including a moon that rose a little early. The barn collapsed just a couple of weeks after this photo was taken and it will never be photographed again.

John Paul Hammerschmidt Falls, Ponca Wilderness, Buffalo National River

It is only fitting that a beautiful waterfall be named after our friend and longtime Congressman who helped create the Buffalo National River. His waterfall is located high in the headwaters of Indian Creek, and the waters eventually flow into the Buffalo.

Dogwood blossoms, Ozarks

What most of us think of as the "flowers" or blossoms of the dogwood tree are actually a set of modified leaves or "bracts." The flowers are in the center of these—all those green and yellow guys like you see here.

Twilight, Lake Grampus Swamp, Ashley County

Swamps. I love swamps. Especially late in the day when colors from the sky mingle with the shapes on the water. I was standing in about two feet of nearly-black water when I took this photograph. Something kept nibbling at my bare toes, but I really didn't want to know what it was.

Sunrise under the great arch, Buzzard Roost Special Interest Area, Ozark National Forest

When the sun reaches its southern-most track in late December, it will rise under this beautiful sandstone arch for several days. The view is blocked the rest of the year as the sun is over to the left/north. It was a chilly ten degrees when I left my truck and hiked two miles before sunrise to reach this location, and I was rewarded with a glorious display.

Love-in-a-mist, Mom's Meadow at Cloudland

This is not exactly a native wildflower to Arkansas, but we have lots of them growing in the little meadow below our cabin so I thought I should include it (the seeds were included in a wildflower mix that we planted). The detail and complexity in this flower is just incredible. And what a terrific name!

Late evening golden light, Little Missouri River, Ouachita National Forest

Sometimes in the evening, just before the sun goes away, there is an incredible play of light and color from surrounding trees that is reflected in water. You have to get down really low, but you can see the blues of the sky, greens from the trees, and the soft gold of sunset, all there swirling in the waters.

Frost flowers and frostweed, Buffalo River Wilderness

Some of the most delicate forms of ice appear as "frost flowers" in early winter, when the temp is down in the teens and twenties. Water and sap are pushed out of the stem of the plant as the cold temps cause the liquid to expand, creating some amazing shapes as they "grow" (notice how the stem has been ripped apart by this action). These ultra-thin wafers of ice are easily crushed, and will melt away as the first rays of sunshine hit them—or will melt in your hand within a few seconds.

Cedar Falls, Petit Jean State Park

Every day spent in the woods taking pictures is special, but once in a while you stumble into pure magic, as was the case on the day I took this photograph. We normally don't have a lot of water in the fall in Arkansas, so a waterfall photo with blazing fall scenery all around is rare. But we had that combination up on Petit Jean Mountain one year, and I got lucky and was there with camera in hand. It rained lightly most of the day, and I hiked around and took hundreds of pictures. Just before dark, as I was leaving to go home, I waded out into the stream and found this scene. I had to work fast because the light was fading, and this was a once-in-a-lifetime shot for me. As it turned out, the six-second exposure that was required was an advantage as it streaked the leaves and foam on the water surface, creating a wonderful interaction with the colorful reflection.

Raindrops after the storm, serviceberry tree

Raindrops are Mother Nature's diamonds. If you want to feel really rich, go outdoors while it is raining. Get down on your hands and knees and crawl around a while and look at all the fancy jewels. You will feel like royalty!

Behold the beautiful pelican.
Its bill can hold more than its belly-can...
—Dixon Merritt

Dardanelle Lock and Dam,
Arkansas River

My bride on Hawksbill Crag, Upper Buffalo Wilderness, Ozark National Forest

This famous rock formation is located about a half mile from our cabin. Every now and then I will holler to my wife and we will run out the door with camera gear in hand—another great light show has begun. She is always a good sport, and willing to become part of the scene—and sometimes even gets a little bit of exercise in too.

Sandstone blocks, moss and lichen, Leatherwood Wilderness, Ozark National Forest

Sometimes you hike into an area expecting one thing, and find something else entirely different. That was the case when I went in to photograph a pair of lovely waterfalls called "The Funnel" inside the Leatherwood Wilderness area. I knew there were dogwood and redbud trees in front of the falls that should be blooming, and I had hoped for high water in the falls from recent rains. When I arrived I found the trees in full bloom, but the waterfalls were very low and the light was terrible. While I waited for the light to change, I explored along the bluffline and literally stumbled onto this scene that reminded me of giant pizza slices. I say "giant" because that center "slice" is about twenty feet across. This shot was taken with an ultra-wide-angle lens in order to get everything in. Those cracks in between the slices were about ten feet deep. I never did get a good shot of the waterfalls and blooming trees, so I guess I will just have to go back next year and try again!

The symphony before the sunrise, from the back deck at Cloudland

It was a frigid winter morning when I crawled out of bed and ran out onto the deck of our cabin to photograph this incredible scene. The vibrant colors were only there for a few minutes, and I must have shot 75 pictures. As the color was fading I began to feel a draft, and realized I was standing there on the frozen deck with bare feet and wearing nothing but my underwear.

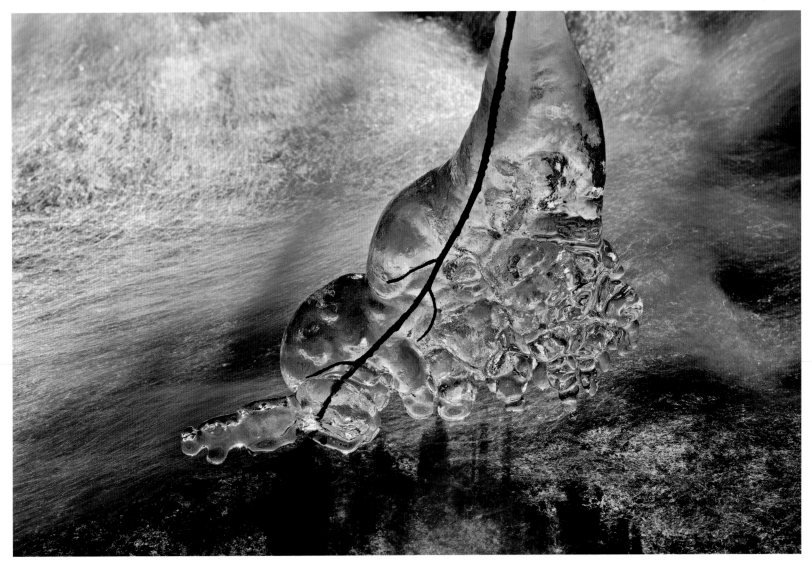

Sunshine dancing on the water and ice, Dug Hollow, Buffalo River Wilderness

If you were insulated with a thick blanket of ice like this branch was, would you be warm? When wandering around with my camera, I often look for places in nature where opposites meet—like the warm golden sunshine and blue ice.

Jack-in-the-pulpit, Dismal Hollow, Ozark National Forest

This is one of the most unusual wildflowers there is, and I often stop, drop to my knees, and see if I can look up under the flap and see who is home.

Red maple leaves during "leaf-fall" on a small stream along the Ozark Highlands Trail, Ozark National Forest

Sometimes in the fall at the peak of color, thousands of leaves all decide to let go and float down to earth at the same time. I call this phenomenon "leaf-fall," and if you are lucky enough to be there when it happens, it is one of the most magical moments you can ever spend outdoors. The fresh leaves cover the forest floor, and create some remarkable scenes.

Morning glories greet the new day, Buffalo River Wilderness

It's five o'clock this morning and the sun is on the rise... John Denver used to sing about the start of a new day. It is when things come alive and smile and everything is fresh and right with the world. No one knows that more than flowers do, and you will always see them perk up at daylight. Early morning is the very best time to be out in the wilderness.

A summer sunrise burns off fog in the deep woods at Cloudland

This is what summer looks like outside our cabin in the morning. First, a thick layer of dense fog engulfs everything. Then a hint of sunshine begins to peek through. Soon the rays burn through the fog and it is like walking through a rain shower of sunshine. It feels good on your face, and gets the day off to a great start!

Wild strawberry blossom and the last frost of the season, Boxley Valley

By the time the heat of late June arrives this flower will have transformed into a tiny morsel of sweetness, if it survives the frost. I read somewhere that while the early bird may get the worm, it is the *second* mouse that gets the cheese! Sometimes being early is not always a great idea.

Falling Water Creek, Ozark National Forest

There is something about this scene that is so fresh and scrubbed clean and inviting—I want to splash right on up the middle of the creek and see where it goes. That is exactly what I was doing when I shot this photo—standing in the water with my tripod, exploring upstream.

"Ice balls" at the base of the Glory Hole, Dismal Creek Special Interest Area, Ozark National Forest (following pages)

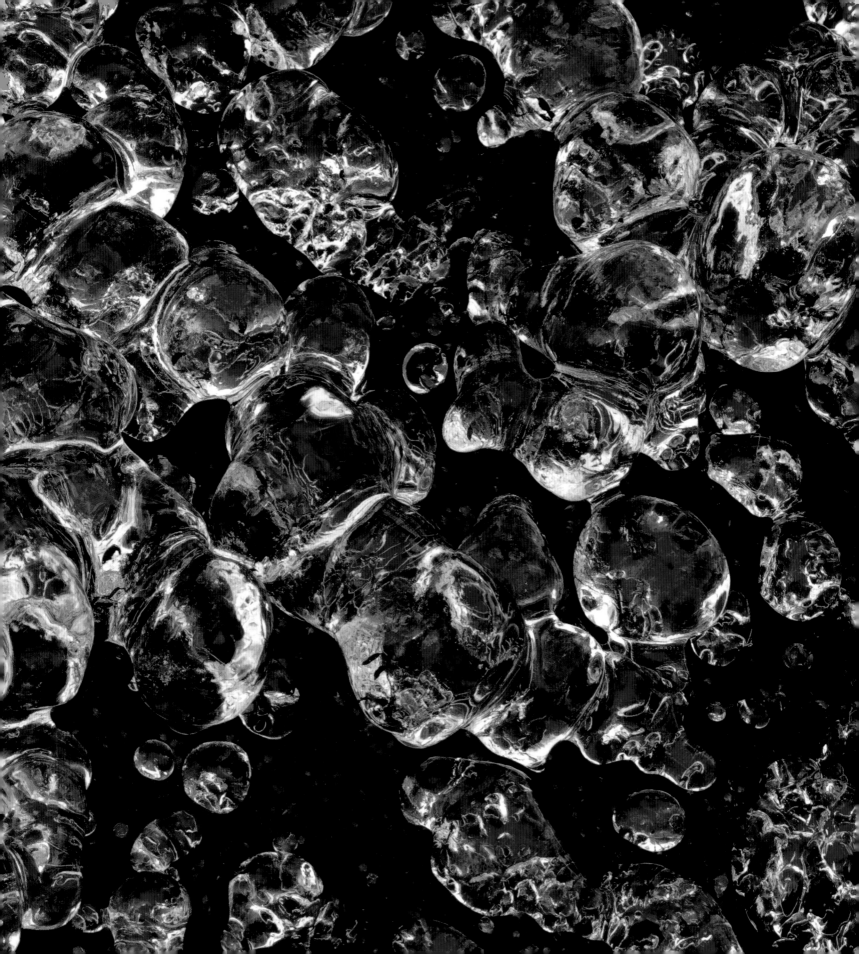

Part Two

There are many terrific wild waterfalls in Arkansas. It was very nice of someone to build a road right next to Falling Water Falls, which is one of the most scenic waterfalls in the state, so that everyone can go see it. The falls has a great deep pool at the base of it, and is used throughout the summer by locals as a swimming hole (note the wooden boards on the tree).

I have photographed this waterfall many times over the years. One of the first times I saw it, I stood at the top of the bluff that the wooden ladder leads too. It was a cold day in February, and my hands were getting numb. As I reached out to remove a polarizing filter from the front of my lens, the filter slipped out of my hands and bounced over the ledge and into the pool below. That water was so clear, I could see right where my filter had come to rest—at the bottom of about six feet of water. Being a poor, starving artist, I was not going home without that expensive filter, so I stripped everything off and went in after it. Mind you, the temp was about 20 degrees, and that water was a wee bit chilly! I got my filter back, but my voice changed a little.

The next time I took pictures there, the water levels were really high and I stood at the base of the falls photographing a pair of kayakers as they went over the falls and plunged into the emerald pool below. *Could you please do that again so I could try a different shutter speed?* Those guys were nuts, and happily went over again and again.

The day that I took this photo, we arrived early in the morning to shoot images for the cover of Glenn Wheeler's **Swimming Holes of the Ozarks** guidebook. We spent a couple of hours working on that job and got a good image, then left and went onto other locations for more shooting. On the way home late in the day, I happened to stop by the falls once again. It was Mother's Day, and having just lost my mom to Alzheimer's, I wanted to spend some quiet time in a beautiful location thinking about this most wonderful lady. She loved nature and always encouraged me to follow my dreams. On this day my dreams were of her, and thinking about how much she would have loved this spot. Even though the light should have been terrible for photos at that time of the day, for some reason the light was quite remarkable—I ran back up to my truck and grabbed my camera gear. This one is for you mom!

Falling Water Falls on Falling Water Creek, Ozark National Forest

The first snow of the season, Whitaker Creek, Buffalo River Wilderness, Ozark National Forest

When snow blankets the forest, everything is still and quiet. You will see me rush out the door to go play. However, I tend to speak in hushed tones, move slowly, and linger for a while when I came across a scene like this one.

Maple tree (double-exposure blur technique), Richland Creek Wilderness, Ozark National Forest

There is a technique that I use sometimes called a "double-exposure blur." Basically all you do is take one photo with your subject in focus, and a second photo with the subject out of focus, or "blurred." The combined image often has a dreamy look to it, and can vary from subtle to dramatic depending on how out of focus or blurred the second exposure is. You will find several examples of this in the book, normally they are close-ups of wildflowers, but once in a while I will do a branch or tree, like this one.

Cardinal flower, Buffalo River Wilderness

This brilliant wildflower is often a shock to your system because they bloom late in the season, after most other wildflowers have faded away. I've spent many a hot August day exploring a dry creekbed and discovered flashes of color that are most welcome.

A very cold morning in the river, Roark Bluff, Ponca Wilderness, Buffalo National River

I have photographed Roark Bluff hundreds of times and wanted to get a different perspective when I made this shot. So I waded out into the river and set up my tripod at the lower end of this long pool, right where the calmness breaks and begins a set of rapids. I stood there for ten minutes making photographs, then realized when I started to pack up and leave that my legs were numb from the frigid water and I could not walk (this was in January). I almost fell head first into the river!

Full moon over Mt. Nebo, Holla Bend National Wildlife Refuge

I think that we were meant to roam around in the moonlight, and I do so every chance I get. There is a unique look to everything—it is more intimate than any other light. And there is music in the moonlight—the softest lullaby you will ever hear. Shhhhh, listen. Stand next to someone under the next full moon and put your arm around them, and you both will smile.

Ozark wake robin along the Lost Valley trail, Buffalo National River

As some flowers get older, their colors get dark and more intense, and I think they have a greater personality as well. Now that I am into the second half of my life, I'm doing the very same thing (I was blonde, now I'm just gray!). The valley floor along this trail is often covered with wildflowers, and it is one of the most spectacular hikes in the state during March and early April. Be careful not to step on any of the old guys!

The legendary sunrise on the Mill Pond, Boxley Valley, Buffalo National River

As I was leaving my cabin early one morning, I saw a hint of color in the east and a layer of clouds. I wanted to photograph sunrise at this famous mill pond in Boxley for years, but had never caught it just right, so I put the pedal to the metal and sped towards Boxley as the colors got brighter. I came to a screaming halt at the pond, holding my breath as I drove up that the winds were calm enough for a reflection, and sure enough, they were. I jumped out, climbed up onto a rock for a better view, set up my tripod, and fired off about 30 shots as the sky and water both lit up. Within two minutes the color began to fade and it was all over. I stood there stunned and breathless, hoping I had "got" it. Later I discovered that dozens of photographers had other versions of this same sunrise, taken from different locations around the state. It is the most photographed sunrise I have ever seen. And oh yes, my version came out!

Unnamed waterfall, Smith Creek Tract, Nature Conservancy

Today I have grown taller
from walking with the trees.
—Karle Wilson Baker

A hike along Cave Mountain Road,
Ozark National Forest

Spider lilies, Desha County

What a perfect name for these flowers! I bet if you turned one of them upside down and placed it on the ground it would run off.

After the sunset, walnut trees, crescent moon, Cave Mountain

These two walnut trees live near our cabin, and for years every time there was color in the evening sky I would race out the door, trying to catch the perfect light to photograph them in silhouette. I think winter trees have a great deal of personality, and their bare branches tell a lot about them. This view reminds me of two lovers sitting close, watching the moonrise.

A group of yellow trout lilies laugh at the photographer, Lost Valley Trail, Buffalo National River

I have this "fisheye" lens that creates a great deal of distortion in the scene, but also provides a very wide view when I really need it. It also allows me to get up close to my subject, yet still see a lot of the scenery in the background. This little group of trout lilies seemed to be laughing at me when I got down on my belly to take their portrait—the ground was wet and muddy and I felt like a wallowing hog (probably looked like one too).

Late afternoon light on the Buffalo River, Boxley Valley

To paint with the colors of nature on a palette of smooth, clear water—what a glorious job the sun has!

Bloodroot, Lost Valley Trail, Buffalo National River (double-exposure blur technique)

Most photographers look for wildflowers that are fully open before they photograph them. I sometimes seek out different stages of their life cycle, just because. This tiny bloodroot flower reminded me of a white rose. For some reason I held my breath while making this picture, not wanting to disturb what seemed like a very quiet and reverent moment.

Ice formation, Dug Hollow, Buffalo River Wilderness

What incredible shapes and patterns have been built here! The ice seems to be reaching out to the water, but no need to rush—it will melt into the river soon enough.

Eastern tiger swallowtail butterfly and clover, Cave Mountain

Have you ever chased a butterfly around the yard trying to get its picture? It is a tough job, but someone has to do it. Being a nature photographer allows you to be a kid again (or did I ever grow up to begin with?).

Low water in the early summertime, Buffalo River Wilderness

These rocks have been rolling and tumbling downstream for eons, coming to rest here, at least for a little while. The next big flood will pick them up and send them to a new home once again, sanding them off a little more along the way.

Lady bug and toothwort, Lost Valley Trail, Buffalo National River (double-exposure blur technique)

Hey ladybug, could you please hold still so I can take your picture? She was most cooperative.

Triple Falls at Camp Orr, Buffalo National River

This is also known as Twin Falls, but since we have so many other "Twins" in Arkansas, and since I've answered the question a hundred times "how come it is called twin when there are three?", I changed the name for my guidebook and all photo captions to Triple Falls. It is one of the most spectacular, easy waterfalls to get to, and photographs pretty well too. I shot this from under an umbrella during a driving rainstorm one day. Seems only natural to photograph waterfalls while it is raining!

Snow makes whiteness where it falls.
The bushes look like popcorn balls.
And places where I always play,
look like somewhere else today.
—Mary Louise Allen

Hawksbill Crag,
Upper Buffalo Wilderness,
Ozark National Forest

Looking out from under a giant boulder, Dug Hollow, Buffalo River Wilderness

I love to crawl under stuff and see what the view is like. There is a GIANT boulder below this unnamed waterfall, and this is the view looking back up at the falls from under the boulder. The stream created by the falls flows under the rock, and there are interesting things to look at under there, but it is pretty dark. I am hopeful that boulders like this won't decide to roll over while I am under them!

The trail to Hawksbill Crag during "leaf-fall," Upper Buffalo River Wilderness, Ozark National Forest

Besides the great beauty of being out during leaf-fall, this photo is a favorite of mine because of its historical significance for me. It is the very last of literally millions of images that I shot on film (and is the only image in this book that was shot on film). I switched to digital cameras soon after, and have never looked back. So I guess you could say this was the path leading me into the future.

Wild honeysuckle, Boxley Valley

Deer just love to munch on wild honeysuckle. The city variety of honeysuckle is mighty tasty too—I use to pinch the head off of one and pull the long stem out *carefully*, and at the very end was a single drop of pure sweetness!

Roark Bluff, Buffalo National River

While standing on the banks of the Buffalo one day with a group of other photographers, someone remarked it would be great if we only had a red canoe to photograph. Out of the blue, this guy appeared upstream and quickly floated right in front of us. He seemed to be in a hurry to get out of our way, but he was, of course, *the* center of focus for us, and we all scrambled to get our cameras set up. I only got three exposures of him before he moved on. Sometimes things just happen at the right time, and you have to be ready for them.

Golden evening sunshine on a snowy landscape, Upper Buffalo Wilderness

Here is a tale of two rivers, one frigid and bathed in warm light, the other hot with cool blue waters; yet both are the same river, one feeding into the other. These two photos were taken on the Buffalo River a couple of miles apart at different times of the year, but at the same time of day (the end of it). Like people, rivers have many different moods and personalities. Variety is indeed the spice of life, and living around the Buffalo River is like eating hot peppers for breakfast!

Summer moonrise over the skinny-dipping hole, Upper Buffalo Wilderness

Who could resist? It was hot and sultry at the end of a long day of bushwhacking through the wilderness in search of visual pleasures for my camera to record. And then I stumbled onto this scene. The cool, deep waters called to me to jump in. But then, if I did, the reflection and the moment would be ruined. Was it my duty as a nature photographer to record the scene; or to heck with it—should I just strip down and jump right in?

Slot canyon on Shop Creek, Buffalo National River

Cattle egret and morning glory, Lake Chicot State Park

Sunrise and cypress trees, Lake Chicot (above)

Cinnamon ferns and sandstone bluff, Dismal Hollow, Ozark National Forest (opposite page)

Skull Bluff on the Buffalo River (following pages)

Part Three

Throughout my entire 30-year photo career the person I have always looked up to the most, who has been the most important influence on my work, and who I consider the greatest wilderness photographer of all time, is Ansel Adams. He is the master of black and white—no one has ever made a fine print better than his. Yet with all of this black and white influence on me, I have never shot nor made any black and white prints. That is, until now.

Ansel was a fabulous photographer for sure, but his genius happened in the darkroom, often spending days perfecting his manipulations on a single print before he was satisfied. While I have spent many moons in my own darkroom, I was always more interested in being outside than in the dark. But now with the digital darkroom, we are able to produce world-class images without ever turning the light switch off, or mixing and inhaling all those nasty chemicals. Now I *am* interested.

Shooting black and white images for me is not really done any differently then my color work—in fact, all of my black and white photos are shot in color to begin with (there is more information/details captured by the camera when you shoot in color). But once I get into the digital darkroom, everything changes. I have infinite control over the tones, contrast and exposure, with precise dodging and burning—Ansel would have killed for a copy of Photoshop, and would have been first in line to get at this computer stuff! The papers I use for my fine art black and white prints are actually more archival than any of Ansel's prints. I will never be able to produce an image as good as Ansel, but it has been a lot of fun trying to follow in his footsteps.

In addition to normal black and white stuff, I have discovered the beauty and pleasure of infrared photography. In the past the results from infrared film were unpredictable and difficult to master. But with a digital camera that I have had converted to capture infrared images, it is almost child's play now. (Oops, I mean **work**, it is all work!) And perhaps the best thing about infrared is the fact that the best time to shoot it is in the middle of a bright sunny day—normally that is the worst time for my color work. Now I can extend my photographic day, and my subject material—some subjects or scenes I would never point a camera at for color make perfect infrared images.

Has it been tough making the transition from color to black and white? Sure. There is a great deal more to learn about and perfect. But I got a jump start on all of it by spending time with two wonderful teachers. George Lepp got me going with infrared, and convinced me that I needed that special infrared camera (and, oh brother, was he right!). And then I spent a magical week in Santa Fe with one of Ansel's former assistants, Carlan Tapp. Carlan is a master black and white printer, but also photographs with more soul than anyone I have ever been around.

So with a nod to Ansel, George, and Carlan, and for the very first time in my career, I present to you a short selection of black and white images (without comments—they will speak for themselves).

Hay field, barn, summer clouds, along Scenic Highway 7, Newton County (infrared)

Beech tree roots, Buffalo National River (sepia-toned)

Cascade above Thunder Canyon, Buffalo National River (Cecil Cove area)

An old cedar tree at sunrise, Buffalo River Wilderness (sepia-toned infrared)

Tea Table Rocks, Home Valley Bluff (infrared)

Sunrise, Buzzard Roost Special Interest Area, Ozark National Forest

Star moss, Buffalo National River (infrared)

Grotto Falls, Leatherwood Creek, Buffalo National River (fisheye lens)

Little stones and bigger stones, Cossatot River State Park Natural Area

Heavy snow and barn on Cave Mountain

Bull skull, Cave Mountain (sepia-toned)

Part Four

Is there a more powerful symbol of freedom than our own American bald eagle? They used to be nearly extinct in Arkansas, but now we have hundreds of them winter here each year. Every time I see one soaring high in the sky, I stop to look and am amazed at the grace and beauty.

This past year I made it a priority to get out and take some eagle photos—never had any success before. I scheduled several trips down to one of the best wildlife areas in the state, Holla Bend National Wildlife Refuge just outside of Russellville. I timed it to coincide with the full moon—exciting images seem to happen around the full moon. Fellow photographer, Larry Roberts, met me and we drove around the refuge before, during, and after sunrise and sunset. We got some great photos of eagles, the predawn light, the moonset, incredible flocks of snow geese, and a bunch of other great subjects. This is a terrific place to go spend some time in the winter if you are interested in winged wildlife (other kinds too).

On one of our trips around the refuge, Larry spotted a mature bald eagle sitting in a tree about a mile away, a tree that was right next to the road. I got my camera gear ready as he drove closer. We held our breaths as we passed directly under the bird—and he stayed put! (We needed to get to the other side of the bird for the best light.) Even before Larry had stopped the truck I was out the door and focused on the giant bird. I almost always use a tripod when shooting anything, but had a feeling there would not be time to use one for this shot, so I just pointed my big lens skyward, set a very high shutter speed, and fired away. Within seconds the bird had had enough of us, and flew off. I got my eagle shot and was a happy camper.

Later in the winter I took Larry to a spot near Bentonville where we saw dozens and dozens of bald eagles, but we were never able to get as close to them. Even though we returned to that eagle mecca many times, I never got a photo as good as this one from Holla Bend. I find it humorous that I can sit and wait for an hour for the wind to stop, or the light to change, often not getting a single good photo. And then in a few quick seconds I get a shot of a lifetime.

Bald eagle and moon, Holla Bend National Wildlife Refuge

Wild azalea, Kings River Falls Natural Area

I went out early one morning in search of azaleas, and found this plant that was lit up by a single shaft of sunshine. The background remained in deep shadow. While I was behind the camera, all I could see were the flowers and leaves—the rest of the world had disappeared into darkness.

Spring runoff, Smith Creek Tract, Nature Conservancy

Where did this water come from? It fell from the sky, ran down the mountain, joined together with a lot of other raindrops, then decided to make friends with the rocks. The water is actually liquid sandpaper, and every drop takes a tiny bit of rock with it on the long journey to the Gulf of Mexico.

Trumpeter swan at Magness Lake near Heber Springs

The gracefulness and beauty of a swan—there is nothing quite like it. There is a flock of them that spend the winter on a private lake in Arkansas. They come back every year, and are quite friendly and willing to pose for photos.

Predawn, Holla Bend National Wildlife Refuge

Like swans, bare trees have a grace and beauty all their own, especially when you sneak up on them and capture a still moment on the water. I am drawn to reflections—they double the visual pleasure.

Pawpaw blossoms, Cave Mountain

I have always remembered the old song from my childhood "way down yonder in the pawpaw patch…" We have several patches of pawpaw trees up here near our cabin, and they produce some of the sweetest fruit you have ever tasted. The blooms are tiny and often difficult to photograph because they are normally high up in the trees. These blooms were on a branch that was bent down from a powerful spring storm that rolled through the night before, and I was able to get right in close to them for this shot. I don't use any sort of artificial light in my work, and what you see here, are the flowers looking directly into the setting sun.

Cedar Falls, sweet gum trees, Petit Jean State Park

Sweet gum trees guard one of the most beautiful waterfalls in Arkansas. They feed off of the constant spray from the thundering water, and put on a great show in the fall.

Multi-colored rocks behind Grotto Falls, Leatherwood Creek, Buffalo National River

I don't know where these rocks came from—they do not look like the normal smooth stones you would find in a stream. I discovered them in the back of an overhanging bluff while taking pictures of the waterfall. I guess they are fresh from the earth and have not had a chance to be worn smooth yet.

Umbrella magnolia blossom in the rain, Dismal Hollow, Ozark National Forest

This is a life-size photo of the largest flower in the forest. When you find a tree full of them in bloom, you will be transported to the tropics, and the fragrance will knock you over.

When we tug at a single thing in nature we find it attached to the rest of the world.
—John Muir

**Cypress trees at dawn,
Lake Chicot**

Fall color and polished stones, Buffalo National River

Fall color and still pools go together. The stones along the bank are all lined up just waiting to be tossed in by a child, young or old.

Umbrella magnolia trees, Dismal Hollow, Ozark National Forest

I believe the tree on the left must be listening to music.

Ozark wake robin along the Lost Valley Trail, Buffalo National River

Wildflowers always seem to be happy, and they live with smiles on all the time. They see a lot going on in the forest from their low vantage points—if you get down on your hands and knees, and get real close, they will tell you a secret.

Hoar frost in the hardwoods, Ozark National Forest

"Hoar frost" develops when it is cold enough to freeze the moisture that is in fog. As the fog drifts through the trees at the higher elevations, the frost forms on the branches, creating some wonderful scenes. We can often see ridge tops from our cabin that are blanketed with a white frosting, while the rest of the hills that are lower and warmer look up and envy the beauty of the ice.

Evening light, Cedar Creek, Petit Jean State Park

Here is another shot that was taken late one evening showing that golden glow on the water. Two legs of my tripod were in the stream, and the camera was so low to the surface of the water that the lens kept getting splashed.

My bride and Eden Falls, Lost Valley, Buffalo National River

I've photographed Eden Falls hundreds of times, and this is my favorite shot of them all. Sometimes the same old view can get a little, well, boring. So you will often see me exploring around all over the place to find a new and different vantage point. My bride, Pamela, was with me on this trip, and I asked her to go "explore" close to the falls so I could use her for scale.

Sunset over Lake Ludwig, Johnson County

What lake have you been standing in? was the question put to me as I got home late one night. My wife knows to expect just about anything from me when I venture out to take photographs. She was correct, I had been standing in a lake, and was covered with mud and slime. As I was driving back home from a trip down south, I began to see some brilliant colors forming in the western sky. I remembered this lake dead ahead along the highway, so I sped on until I reached it, then pulled over and jumped out. I literally ran to the edge of the lake as the colors intensified above—and there was no wind so the reflections were great. Much to my horror the sides of the lake were covered with tall weeds, and I could not find a spot along the bank with a clear view out into the water. The color was just incredible, but I knew it would only last moments longer. So what the heck, I just walked right on in, clothes and shoes and all, until I got as deep as I dared (about chest deep). The tripod sank into the mud, and the camera was just above the surface of the water. I had to remain still while I worked the camera so as not to create ripples and mess up the reflection. I cursed every time a fish jumped. The colors you see here are real—it was one of the most incredible displays of color I have ever seen in nature.

Umbrella magnolia blossom, Buffalo River Wilderness

Most of these flowers bloom high up in the tree, and you rarely get to look them in the eye. But every now and then a young tree will have giant blooms, so heavy in fact that the weight of them bends the tree over and the blooms get really low to the ground.

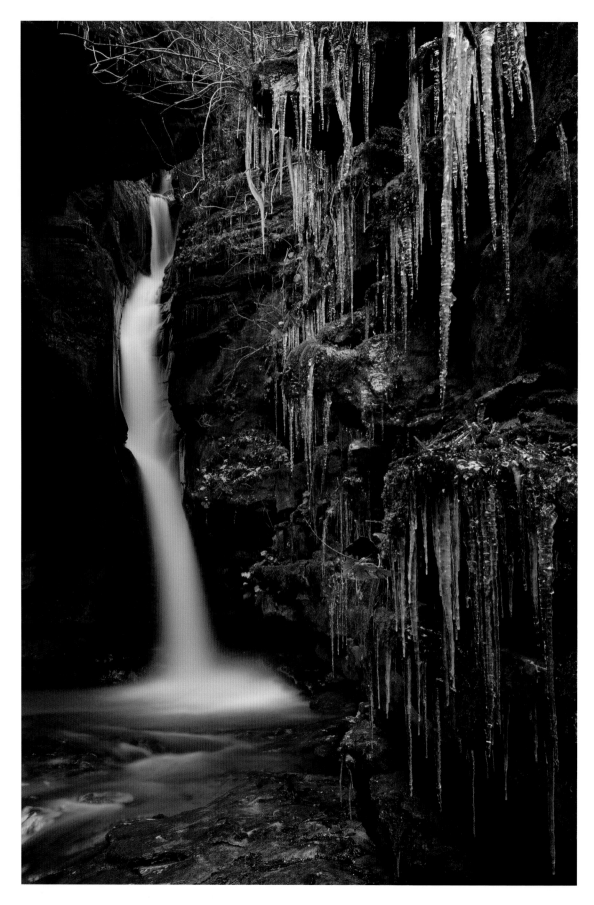

A friendly copperhead, Buffalo River Wilderness

During one of my photo workshops on a chilly morning in April my assistant, Glenn Wheeler, informed me that three of us had just walked right on top of this copperhead! The temperature was so cool that the snake was not moving too fast. Glenn, who is a great photographer in his own right, picked up the copperhead and placed it on a large rock, right next to where we were making photographs of a beautiful waterfall. Mr. Snake remained on that rock for a full hour, and seemed to be quite happy to pose for photos. Note to self: when picking workshop assistants, find one that is a good snake wrangler too!

Thunder Canyon Falls, Buffalo National River (Cecil Cove area)

This is one of many great hidden and previously unnamed waterfalls that are in my *Arkansas Waterfalls Guidebook.* As I first approached it, I could hear what I thought was thunder, but it turned out to be the sound of the waterfall—hence the name. This falls is actually more than 70 feet tall, much of it hidden up in the rocks above.

**Autumn reflections,
Buffalo National River**

There are moments when silence is paradise
and everything falls into place.

Moss, water and blue sky, behind Haley Falls, Upper Buffalo Wilderness, Ozark National Forest

Each time I approach a waterfall I try to look for the most interesting ways to photograph it—and that is not always from the front! You'll see me back behind them quite often, like I was when I shot this scene. I used a long lens to isolate the detail in the moss and water against the blue afternoon sky. Then I shot a series of images using different shutter speeds—which blurred the water in different ways. You never know exactly which one is going to work, if any, but I think this one calls to mind the scene as I witnessed it.

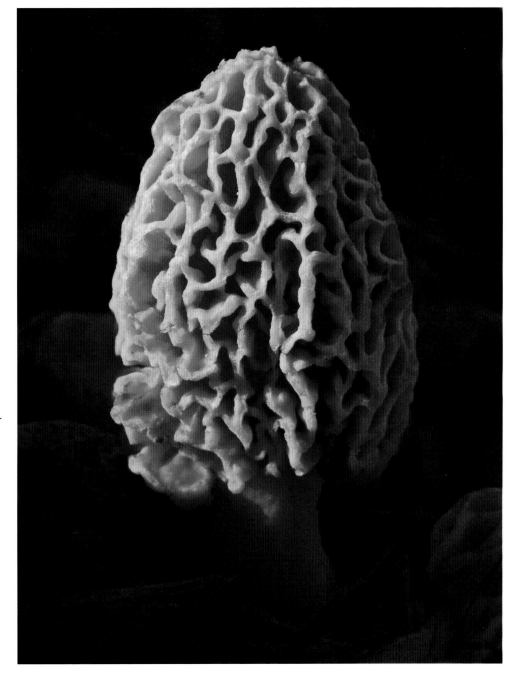

Morel mushroom at Cloudland

Unlike most of the world, I can't stand the taste of mushrooms, and have never paid much attention to them in the wild before. However, now that my mother-in-law loves morels, I pay particular attention to them when they pop up in the spring. This one disappeared a few moments after I took its picture.

Sweet gum tree in the wind, Cedar Creek, Petit Jean State Park

Seems like I spend half of my time waiting for the wind to stop so that I can capture sharp details in the subjects I photograph. Sometimes the wind will never stop, and you either have to give up and go home, or use it to your advantage. I used a long shutter speed here to let the blowing branches paint a picture of themselves.

Backlit bloodroot, Buffalo River Wilderness

Flowers and leaves look really nice when backlit—it tends to bring out details that you could never see otherwise. This is the very first "real" photograph that I took with a digital camera, while on a hike down to my favorite swimming hole—or actually it was on the way back UP the hill to the cabin after an afternoon of swimming. The evening sun was dropping low and really lighting up this flower and its leaf. The single leaf on the bloodroot plant is huge, with an unmistakable shape. You normally can't photograph them backlit since they grow so low to the ground, but this guy was standing straight up in the air and waving at me.

Flowering dogwood, Petit Jean State Park

Can you spot the upside-down ant that is hiding behind one of the flowers? If you look close at most flowering species you will find many little critters in there working to make a living. By the way, there is a spider hiding in the showy orchis on page one—did you see it?

Almost sunset from Flatside Pinnacle, Flatside Wilderness, Ouachita National Forest (Forked Mountain in the distance)

It is a short but steep hike up to the top of Flatside Pinnacle, and the view from there is just wonderful. It looks out over one of the largest wilderness areas in Arkansas, and has a great view to the west. That is my favorite mountain in all of Arkansas off in the distance, Forked Mountain. There is another shot of that same mountain that I took from the base of it on page 16.

The first wildflower of spring at Cloudland, a trout lily

There are thousands of trout lilies on our property, but this very flower pictured above is the first one to pop up out of the leaves and bloom every spring, year in and year out. He lives right at the edge of a trail, and we begin looking for him in early February. Once he is up and basks in the sunshine for a while, he will call out to the others that it is time to wake up, and the forest floor comes alive with trout.

View of the river from Bee Bluff, Buffalo National River

Some people call me an old goat. I'm not sure if it is because of my looks, or the fact that I like to hang out on the top of tall blufflines—I find the view is much better from up there. As you might imagine from looking at this photograph, I was hanging out over the edge of this bluff in order to get the shot.

123

Luna moth on sandstone, Buffalo River Wilderness (above, almost actual size)
How many eyes does it take to navigate the night sky—this guy must be a great flyer! These moths are nearly as large as your hand, and you can't help but notice when one is in the area. It is always a special treat for us to find one.

Unnamed falls, Smith Creek Tract, Nature Conservancy (opposite page)
Waterfalls enjoy life and seem to spend most of their time dancing. I want to be a waterfall when I grow up!

Early morning fog in the deep woods, Buffalo River Wilderness (following pages)

Photo Notes

As you can see from the list of photos on the right, I've been shooting mostly Canon digital cameras for the past couple of years, and almost all of the images in this book were shot with them (my very last exposure on film is also included). Several of the images were taken with high-resolution point-and-shoot cameras, which I find quite useful when I don't want to lug around all of my "real" camera gear. With all of the lenses I carry these days my camera bag tops 50 pounds, not counting my tripod, which I almost always use.

My lenses range from a 15mm fisheye to a 400mm telephoto. My most favorite lens of all lately has been the 180mm macro lens—you will see many flower shots done with it in this book. I just love getting in really close and personal to those beauties! Besides the very best Canon "L" lenses, I also use several old-world, manual focus Zeiss German lenses. These lenses are more difficult and slower to use, but I find they produce some quite lovely images.

It is great to be able to justify using the finest photographic equipment in the world (*Honey, I really <u>need</u> this new lens for my next book project!*). But the truth is that you can create incredible photographs with cheap camera gear; you can also take terrible images with the very best and most expensive stuff. It really has more to do with technique than equipment. I teach photography workshops throughout the year and that is one thing we see over and over again—it is not the equipment, but the photographer that is most important.

Filters, manipulation, faking—I tend to shy away from all three. The only filters I use are polarizing filters, both a normal one and a special blue/gold polarizer that I sometimes use for unique lighting situations (the blue or gold light is there naturally, this filter simply enhances it a little bit). That's it. I do a minimum of processing in the computer, with the goal of reproducing the scene as I saw it, not making up stuff. I don't use any sort of artificial light, however I do try to control light for macro shots, using reflectors to bounce light up into flowers, and/or casting shadows behind them to darken the background (some flower photos here look like they were shot in a studio—yup, the outdoor studio! It is all a matter of controlling the light and the background).

The best advice I can give anyone who wants to make great images is to get out and shoot with the camera you have, and do so early and late in the day when the light is golden. Take lots of photos—the 113 shots in this book came from more than 30,000 that I made in two years. The most important thing is to enjoy creating your art, and being in the great outdoors!

Trumpeter swans, Magness Lake near Heber Springs

Page #	Camera and lens
1	Canon 1Ds Mark II, 180mm macro
2	Canon 20D, 70mm zoom
5	Canon 1Ds Mark II, 180mm macro
6–7	Canon 10D, 30mm zoom
9	Canon 1Ds Mark II, 90mm tilt/shift
11	Canon 1Ds Mark II, 180mm macro
12	Canon 1Ds Mark II, Zeiss 21mm, polarizer
13	Canon 10D, 70mm zoom
14	Canon 1Ds, 32mm zoom
15	Canon 1Ds, 180mm macro
16	Canon 1Ds Mark II, Zeiss 35mm zoom, blue/gold polarizer
17	Canon 1Ds, 180mm macro
18-19	Canon 1Ds, 163mm zoom
20	Canon 1Ds Mark II, 400mm, polarizer
21	Canon 1Ds Mark II, Zeiss 35mm zoom, polarizer
22	Canon 1Ds Mark II, 180mm macro
23	Canon 1Ds Mark II, 35mm Zeiss zoom
24	Canon 1Ds Mark II, 180mm macro
25	Canon 1Ds Mark II, 17mm zoom
26	Canon 1Ds Mark II, Zeiss 28mm, blue/gold polarizer
27	Canon 10D, 50mm macro
28	Canon 20D, 30mm zoom
29	Minolta DiMage 7, 50mm macro zoom
30-31	Canon 1Ds Mark II, 400mm, blue/gold polarizer
32	Canon 1Ds, 70mm zoom, polarizer
33	Canon 1Ds Mark II, Zeiss 21mm, polarizer
34	Canon 1Ds, 70mm zoom
35	Canon 1Ds Mark II, 180mm macro, blue/gold polarizer
36	Canon 1Ds Mark II, 180mm macro
37	Canon 20D, 40mm zoom, polarizer
38	Canon 1Ds, 180mm macro
39	Minolta DiMage 7, 27mm zoom
40	Canon 1Ds Mark II, 180mm macro
41	Canon 1Ds, 35mm zoom, polarizer
42-43	Canon 1Ds, 180mm macro, polarizer
45	Canon 1Ds, 43mm zoom, blue/gold polarizer
46	Canon 1Ds Mark II, 100mm macro
47	Canon 1Ds, 45mm zoom
48	Minolta DiMage A2, 51mm macro zoom
49	Canon 1Ds, 35mm, polarizer
50	Canon 1Ds Mark II, 200mm
51	Canon 1Ds Mark II, 180mm macro
52	Canon 1Ds Mark II, Zeiss 21mm
53	Canon 1Ds Mark II, Zeiss 35mm zoom, polarizer
54-55	Canon 1Ds, 59mm zoom
56	Canon 1Ds Mark II, 180mm macro, polarizer
57	Canon 1Ds, 43mm zoom
58	Canon 1Ds Mark II, 15mm fisheye
59	Canon 1Ds, 48mm zoom, polarizer
60	Canon 1Ds Mark II, 180mm macro
61	Canon 1Ds Mark II, 100mm macro, blue/gold polarizer
62	Minolta DiMage 7, 50mm macro
63	Canon 1Ds Mark II, 90mm tilt/shift, polarizer
64	Canon 1Ds Mark II, Zeiss 35mm
65	Canon 1Ds Mark II, 180mm macro
66-67	Canon 1Ds Mark II, 24mm zoom
68	Contax RTS III, Zeiss 28mm, Velvia 50 FILM!
69	Canon 1Ds, 24mm zoom, polarizer
70	Canon 1Ds Mark II, 180mm macro
71	Canon 1Ds, 45mm zoom
72	Canon 1Ds Mark II, 100mm macro, polarizer
73	Canon 1Ds Mark II, Zeiss 28mm
74	Canon 1Ds Mark II, 400mm
75	Canon 1Ds Mark II, 15mm fisheye
76	Canon 1Ds Mark II, Zeiss 28mm, polarizer
77	Canon 1Ds Mark II, 90mm tilt/shift
78-79	Canon 1Ds, 70mm zoom, polarizer
81	Canon 60D (modified for infrared), 17mm zoom
82	Canon 10D, 29mm zoom, polarizer
83	Canon 1Ds Mark II, 45mm tilt/shift, polarizer
84	Canon 60D (modified for infrared), 17mm zoom
85	Canon 60D (modified for infrared), 20mm zoom
86	Canon 1Ds, 17mm zoom
87	Canon 60D (modified for infrared), 180mm macro
88	Canon 1Ds Mark II, 15mm fisheye
89	Canon 1Ds Mark II, 45mm tilt/shift
90	Canon 1Ds Mark II, 180mm macro
91	Canon 1Ds Mark II, Zeiss 28mm
93	Canon 1Ds Mark II, 400mm, polarizer
94	Canon 1Ds Mark II, 180mm macro
95	Canon 1Ds Mark II, Zeiss 21mm, polarizer
96	Canon 1Ds Mark II, 70mm zoom
97	Canon 1Ds, 400mm, polarizer
98	Canon 20D, 51mm zoom, polarizer
99	Canon 1Ds Mark II, 180mm macro
100	Canon 1Ds Mark II, Zeiss 35mm macro, polarizer
101	Canon 1Ds Mark II, 180mm macro
102-103	Canon 1Ds Mark II, Zeiss 50mm zoom
104	Canon 1Ds, 58mm zoom, polarizer
105	Canon 1Ds Mark II, Zeiss 70mm zoom, polarizer
106	Canon 1Ds Mark II, 180mm macro
107	Canon 1Ds, 25mm zoom, polarizer
108	Canon 1Ds Mark II, Zeiss 28mm, blue/gold polarizer
109	Canon 1Ds Mark II, Zeiss 35mm zoom, polarizer
110	Canon 20D, 21mm zoom
111	Canon 1Ds, 180mm macro
112	Canon 1Ds Mark II, 45mm tilt/shift, polarizer
113	Canon 1Ds, 180mm macro
114-115	Canon 1Ds, 59mm zoom, polarizer
116	Canon 1Ds Mark II, 180mm macro
117	Minolta DiMage 7, 50mm macro
118	Canon 20D, 42mm zoom, polarizer
119	Minolta DiMage 7, 43mm macro zoom
120	Canon 1Ds Mark II, 180mm macro
121	Canon 1Ds, 200mm zoom
122	Canon 1Ds, 35mm zoom, polarizer
123	Canon 1Ds Mark II, 180mm macro
124	Canon 1Ds Mark II, 180mm macro
125	Canon 1Ds Mark II, Zeiss 35mm zoom
126-127	Canon 1Ds, 52mm zoom, polarizer
128	Canon 1Ds, 400mm, polarizer
131	Olympus D560, 12mm zoom
132	Canon 10D, 300mm zoom

About the Photographer

Tim Ernst (that's me!) lives in a log cabin called Cloudland in the middle of the Buffalo River Wilderness in Newton County, Arkansas, with his wife, Pamela, and daughter, Amber.

Seems like I have been taking pictures all of my life, but it has really only been for the past 30 years (I just turned 50). I was 19 when I first pointed a telephoto lens at a gorgeous sunset and realized that was what I needed to do in life. Within a few months of that sunset I started my own wildlife photography business—taking party pictures of sorority girls at the University of Arkansas. While that type of work was a lot of fun and put food on the table, I really longed to be outdoors, and so five years later I sold my photo business and started to pursue other wild things to photograph.

Over the next twenty-something years I spent a great deal of time out in the woods, chasing sunsets, exploring rivers and streams, climbing mountains, getting splashed by waterfalls, and running from big bull elk. I set my tripod legs down in more than 40 states, from below sea level to up above 14,000 feet. I shot more than a couple million photographs on slide film in that time, saw things I had only dreamed of, nearly died every now and then, and grew up a lot. It was a lot of work, but more than a lifetime of fun as well. To put gas in my tank, I sold images to most of the major nature publications in the country, including **National Geographic, Audubon, Backpacker, Outdoor Photographer, Outside, Natural History, Country,** and dozens of other magazines, plus **The New York Times,** Sierra Club calendars, Hallmark cards and calendars, Readers Digest books, and on and on. Along the way I managed to start a publishing business for the hiking trail guidebooks I was writing, and published five coffee-table picture books of my nature photography collections as well, most of them all-Arkansas books (including the original **Arkansas Portfolio** in 1994).

By the time the millennium arrived, my photo career was beginning to wind down. I built a log cabin and moved out into the middle of the wilderness at a place I called Cloudland. Then I sold all of my camera equipment. I was a retired, or should I say washed up, nature photographer. Pretty soon I met the love of my life, Pamela, and she convinced me that I needed to get off the deck and get back out there and take pictures again! I have been doing quite a bit of that ever since. All of the images in this book were made in the past couple of years, and are the direct result of her encouragement. But before I could get back into the groove, I had to start all over again. Film had died, and computers were taking over.

My move into digital photography hit me in the face like a ton of bricks. I literally had to start at ground zero as I knew nothing about it, and there was a great deal to learn. It took me nearly a full year of very intensive study before I got a handle on the finer points of the craft—not so much how to take photos—but how to process the digital images in a way that kept them looking like photographs and not something that was produced inside of a computer. And now for the very first time in my career, I am able to produce photographic prints that are as close to the actual scene as I saw it, than anything possible in the past. It has been quite exciting, and the quality with the latest camera equipment and printing techniques is nothing short of amazing. But all of this is something that requires me to keep on the cutting edge, since the technology continues to change at a rapid pace. Thank goodness my lovely bride allows me to keep up and purchase all the toys (oops, I mean *tools*) that I need.

Along with the digital revolution came the need to educate other photographers about it all—everyone has to start from scratch now, and it can get overwhelming in a hurry. That is good news for me since I teach digital photography workshops! And besides showing folks how to get the best quality out of whatever camera system they happen to be using, I help students navigate through the maze of the digital workflow, a workflow that can get the best of anyone if they don't know how to keep it simple and efficient. We have photography workshops at our wilderness cabin throughout the year. It is great fun for me to see so many advance so far in so little time. The only problem I have with all this—now having taught both film and digital workshops here in Arkansas for nearly twenty years to hundreds of photographers—is the fact that so many of my students are now great photographers, and their competition is getting stiff!

Our publishing business consumes a great deal of our time these days. Lots of folks think we get pretty lazy out here in the woods, but really we put in much more than a normal work week (often double that), and run a busy publishing and distribution business out of our cabin. Thank goodness UPS can find us! My future plans are to continue to take pictures, teach workshops, write, and enjoy my family and the incredible wilderness we call home for at least another 50 years. By the way, if you would like to keep up with all this, and want to read about the adventures surrounding many of the photos in this book, take a look at my online **Cloudland Journal**, where I have been keeping a record of life in the wilderness since 1998—www.Cloudland.net.

Other books by Tim Ernst

Arkansas Portfolio picture book
Wilderness Reflections picture book
Buffalo River Wilderness picture book
Arkansas Spring picture book
Arkansas Wilderness picture book

Arkansas Hiking Trails guidebook
Arkansas Waterfalls guidebook
Ozark Highlands Trail guidebook
Buffalo River Hiking Trails guidebook
Ouachita Trail guidebook
Arkansas Dayhikes For Kids and Families (Pam wrote most of this one!)
The Search For Haley

The old man at 50, with his cameras, on the back deck of the Cloudland cabin. Photo by Pamela Ernst

Bull elk in summer velvet, Boxley Valley (following page)

The End!